PREDATOR vs. PREY

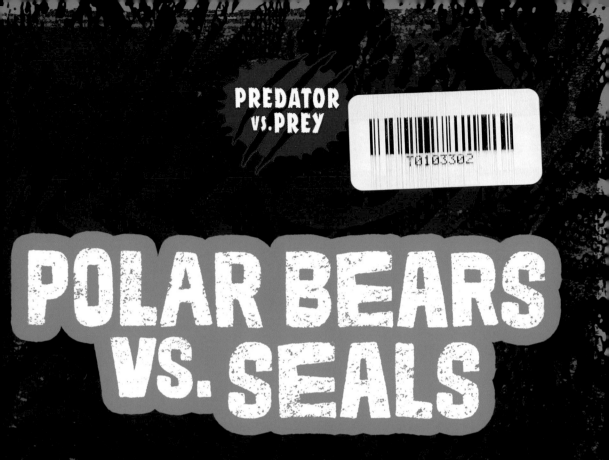

POLAR BEARS VS. SEALS

FOOD CHAIN FIGHTS

SARAH ROGGIO

Lerner Publications ◆ Minneapolis

To Captain, my Captain—I'm so lucky to be your First Mate.

Lerner Publications Company
An imprint of Lerner Publishing Group, Inc.
241 First Avenue North
Minneapolis, MN 55401 USA

For reading levels and more information, look up this title at www.lernerbooks.com.

Main body text set in Aptifer Sans LT Pro.
Typeface provided by Linotype AG.

Editor: Cole Nelson **Designer:** Kim Morales **Photo Editor:** Nicole Berglund
Lerner team: Martha Kranes

Library of Congress Cataloging-in-Publication Data

Names: Roggio, Sarah, author.
Title: Polar bears vs. seals : food chain fights / Sarah Roggio.
Other titles: Polar bears versus seals
Description: Minneapolis : Lerner Publications, [2025] | Series: Predator vs. prey | Includes
    bibliographical references and index. | Audience: Ages 8–11 | Audience: Grades 4–6 | Summary:
    "Polar bears stalk the Arctic ice hunting for seals swimming below. But seals are fast, sneaky,
    and smart. Learn how these creatures survive the icy cold and decide for yourself who rules the
    Arctic"— Provided by publisher.
Identifiers: LCCN 2023043445 (print) | LCCN 2023043446 (ebook) | ISBN 9798765626771 (library
    binding) | ISBN 9798765629406 (paperback) | ISBN 9798765636282 (epub)
Subjects: LCSH: Polar bear—Juvenile literature. | Ringed seal—Juvenile literature. | Predation
    (Biology)—Juvenile literature. | Camouflage (Biology)—Juvenile literature. | Animal defenses—
    Juvenile literature. | Food chains (Ecology)—Juvenile literature.
Classification: LCC QL737.C27 R64 2025 (print) | LCC QL737.C27 (ebook) | DDC 599.786—dc23/
    eng/20231204

LC record available at https://lccn.loc.gov/2023043445
LC ebook record available at https://lccn.loc.gov/2023043446

Manufactured in the United States of America
1-1010124-52008-2/9/2024

TABLE OF CONTENTS

CHAPTER 1
CLASH IN THE ARCTIC

IT IS A FREEZING COLD DAY IN NORTHERN CANADA. This area is next to the Arctic Ocean. Many large, flat pieces of ice called floes float in the Arctic Ocean.

A ringed seal swims below one of these ice floes. This seal is looking for one of the holes it dug in the ice earlier this winter. It needs to find a hole where it can come up for air.

LOOK OUT! A polar bear is walking across the ice. This marine mammal is using camouflage to sneak up on its prey. Its white fur blends in with the snowy scene. The polar bear picks a seal hole in the ice. It stands perfectly still next to this hole, waiting to see if the ringed seal will surface here.

A ringed seal rests on an ice floe in the Arctic Ocean.

Below the ice, the ringed seal must choose a hole where it will come up. It needs air soon. But will it pick a safe spot to take a breath? Or will the polar bear catch its prey? Let's find out!

Polar bears are slow but stalk their prey patiently.

POLAR BEAR STATS

AVERAGE SIZE: 8 feet (2.4 m) tall for females; 10 feet (3 m) tall for males

AVERAGE WEIGHT: 550 pounds (250 kg) for females; 1,500 pounds (680 kg) for males

AVERAGE SPEED: 25 miles (40 km) per hour when running; 6 miles (10 km) per hour when swimming

RINGED SEAL STATS

AVERAGE SIZE: 4 feet (1.2 m) long

AVERAGE WEIGHT: 110 to 240 pounds (50 to 109 kg) in winter, when they are heaviest

AVERAGE SWIMMING SPEED: 6 to 19 miles (10 to 31 km) per hour

CHAPTER 2

POLAR BEARS VS. RINGED SEALS

POLAR BEARS AND RINGED SEALS SHARE THE SAME HABITAT. They live in the Arctic. The Arctic is the region near the North Pole. It includes the US state of Alaska. It also includes the northern parts of several countries such as Canada.

The Arctic Ocean has many ice floes. Polar bears hunt ringed seals on top of the ice. Ringed seals hide from polar bears below the ice.

DIET AND HUNTING HABITS

Polar bears are carnivores. They hunt alone. They mostly hunt seals. But they also eat geese, bird eggs, fish, and small mammals. In the spring, polar bears hunt newborn ringed seal pups. The pups are easy prey because they are born on top of ice floes. Polar bears need the seals' fat to help them get ready for winter.

Ringed seals are also carnivores. They hunt alone in the Arctic Ocean. They mostly eat fish, such as cod. They also eat crustaceans, such as shrimp.

Polar bears spend their time hunting on ice floes and swimming in Arctic waters.

GOING FOR A SWIM

Polar bears are the only bears that are called marine mammals. They spend most of their lives in the Arctic Ocean.

SIZE

Polar bears are huge animals. Fully grown polar bears stand up to 10 feet (3 m) tall. They use more than twice as much energy as most mammals just to move. They spend most of their time resting. Newborn polar bear cubs weigh 1 to 2 pounds (0.5 to 0.9 kg).

A polar bear adult and cub walking along the shore

GROLAR BEAR OR PIZZLY?

Some polar bears and grizzly bears meet and have cubs together in the Arctic. Scientists have called their babies many names, including grolar bears and pizzlies.

Ringed seals make lots of blubber to stay warm in the Arctic winter.

Ringed seals are the smallest type of seal, only around 4 feet (1.2 m) long. Both male and female ringed seals gain weight in the winter and spring. Their bodies make extra blubber to keep them warm. Newborn seal pups weigh around 10 pounds (4.5 kg).

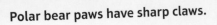

Polar bear paws have sharp claws.

STRENGTH

Polar bears have paws three times the size of an adult human hand! Their paws help spread out their weight when they walk on all fours, so they won't break through the ice. Polar bears can also stand up to walk using their muscular hind legs.

WHY ARE THEY CALLED RINGED SEALS?

Ringed seals get their name from the pattern on their fur coats. Their gray backs are covered in black spots that have rings around them.

Ringed seals have strong, sharp claws on their flippers. They use these claws to dig breathing holes in Arctic ice. They can dig through ice up to 7 feet (2.1 m) thick.

Ringed seals use their flippers to dig through ice and swim underwater.

SPEED

Polar bears walk slowly while swinging their heads from side to side. They also can run for short distances. Their fastest speed on land is 25 miles (40 km) per hour. But most land animals are too fast for polar bears to catch.

A polar bear racing across Arctic ice

Ringed seals swim to hunt prey and hide from predators.

Ringed seals learn how to dive fast as pups to avoid predators. They move their rear flippers back and forth like a fish to push through the water. On ice floes, they use their front flippers to help push their bodies forward as they bounce across the surface.

RINGED SEAL PUPS GROW UP FAST

A mother ringed seal nurses her pup for two months. The pup grows quickly in these two months. Then the pup lives the rest of its life alone.

Some polar bears can swim for days with short rests on ice floes.

AGILITY

Polar bears have rough pads on their paws to help them grip the slippery ice when they walk. They also have webbing between their toes to help them swim.

POLAR BEARS PACK ON THE POUNDS

Polar bears can eat up to 100 pounds (45 kg) of seal blubber at one time! They need this fat to stay warm and well fed through the winter.

Ringed seals can dive up to 300 feet (91 m) deep to find food. They can race through the water at up to 19 miles (31 km) per hour, but on ice they slow to a crawl of about 1 mile (1.6 km) per hour.

A ringed seal prepares to dive into the ocean.

ATTACK AND DEFENSE STYLES

Male polar bears will fight other male polar bears to steal their food or protect their territory during mating season. They growl and shove each other with their huge front paws while trying to bite each other's necks.

Polar bears can fight on all fours and on their hind legs.

Male ringed seals sometimes fight over breathing holes.

Male ringed seals fight each other underwater near breathing holes during the mating season. They try to keep other males away from breathing holes near the snow dens where their babies were born. Females build snow dens to protect their pups and defend them fiercely.

POLAR BEAR SKIN AND FUR

Polar bears only look white because their outer layer of fur reflects light. Their skin is black. The white fur helps polar bears blend in with their snowy surroundings.

Polar bears can wait many hours for prey to appear.

KEY WEAPONS

Polar bears can stand still for a long time while waiting for seals to surface out of the water. Then they pounce on their prey and attack with their sharp teeth and claws.

MALE RINGED SEALS CAN STINK

In the spring, mating males give off a scent that smells like kerosene fuel. Polar bears avoid eating these seals because they taste bad.

Carving breathing holes in ice helps seals stay underwater longer. This allows them to hide below large sections of ice to avoid polar bears. Ringed seals can stay underwater for up to forty-five minutes.

Ringed seals learn to swim soon after they are born.

WEAKNESSES

Polar bears eat animals other than ringed seals. But they mostly need to eat seals to get enough fat for their bodies. It's hard work for polar bears to catch ringed seals. Their prey usually get away because polar bears are slow. In fact, polar bears catch their prey less than 2 percent of the time.

Like ringed seals, polar bears also eat fish.

Ringed seals mostly live alone, but they gather during mating season.

Ringed seals must be on top of the ice for long periods of time. They give birth to one seal pup per year, and they raise their babies on top of the ice. They also shed their hair each year and must sit on the ice while new hair grows. Polar bears can attack them during these times.

RINGED SEALS HAVE NO EARS

Ringed seals do not have outer ears as humans do. Instead, they have ear holes on the sides of their heads that allow them to hear.

CHAPTER 3
WHICH ANIMAL WILL WIN?

THE RINGED SEAL SELECTS A HOLE IN THE ICE WHERE IT WILL SURFACE. But the seal knows that a polar bear may be waiting nearby to strike. So first it sends up air bubbles through the hole. If no polar bear pounces in response, the seal will guess that the hole is safe.

Above this hole, the polar bear sees these air bubbles rise. But it knows this is a test. So it stays still. A polar bear can wait for hours or even days. But this ringed seal is out

A polar bear pulling a ringed seal out of the water

of time. It must get air now. The seal has seen no sign of a polar bear. So it swims to the surface.

The polar bear spots the seal. It plunges its head and front paws into the hole. It grabs the seal and pulls it up onto the ice. The polar bear has its meal.

RULER OF THE HABITAT

Both polar bears and ringed seals can be prey for humans. Indigenous peoples in Canada have hunted both animals for thousands of years. They eat the animals' meat. They are careful not to hunt too many polar bears or seals. The biggest threat to both animals is loss of sea ice. Less sea ice forms in their habitat than it once did. This is due to the Arctic region getting warmer in recent years. Conservation groups are working to protect both animals and their shrinking habitat.

An Inuit hunter wearing traditional hunting clothes

Polar bears and ringed seals play a dangerous game of hide-and-seek on the Arctic ice. Today the polar bear's patience helped it win this risky game. The seal tried to check for threats. But the polar bear just kept waiting. For now, the polar bear rules the Arctic.

Polar bears and ringed seals need ice to live and hunt on.

PREDATOR VS. PREY: HEAD-TO-HEAD

POLAR BEAR
- Rough footpads grip the ice.
- White fur blends into Arctic surroundings.

SEAL

- Sharp claws cut through ice.
- Strong flippers help with deep dives.

GLOSSARY

blubber: the fat of marine mammals

camouflage: how an animal hides by blending in with its surroundings

carnivore: an animal that eats other animals

conservation: a careful preservation or protection of something, such as a natural resource

crustacean: a water-dwelling animal that has a segmented body such as a shrimp or a lobster

habitat: the place where a plant or animal naturally lives or grows

Indigenous: the first people to live in an area

mammal: warm-blooded animals that nourish their young with milk and have skin usually covered with hair

marine: of or relating to the sea

predator: an animal that hunts other animals to eat

prey: an animal hunted by another animal for food

LEARN MORE

Kiddle: Ringed Seal Facts for Kids
https://kids.kiddle.co/Ringed_seal

Klepinger, Teresa. *Grizzly Bear vs. Polar Bear*. Minneapolis: Kaleidoscope, 2022.

National Geographic Kids: Polar Bear
https://kids.nationalgeographic.com/animals/mammals/facts/polar-bear

National Geographic Kids: Polar Habitat
https://kids.nationalgeographic.com/nature/habitats/article/polar

Starr, Abbe L. *Arctic Ice Loss*. Minneapolis: Lerner Publications, 2023.

Taylor, Charlotte. *Polar Bears: Carnivores of the Arctic*. New York: Enslow, 2022.

INDEX

PHOTO ACKNOWLEDGMENTS

Image credits: MB Photography/Getty Images, pp. 4–5; KenCanning/Getty Images, p. 6; Zhiltsov Alexandr/Shutterstock , p. 7 (top); USO/Getty Images, pp. 7 (bottom), 18, 19; Paul Souders/Getty Images, pp. 8–9, 10, 11, 13, 16, 17, 29; Stefan_Redel/Getty Images, p. 12; by wildestanimal/Getty Images, p. 14; karenfoleyphotography/Getty Images, p. 15; Scott Frew/500px/ Getty Images, p. 20; KAZUHIRO NOGI/Getty Images, p. 21; drisley77/Getty Images, p. 22; stockcam/Getty Images, p. 23; Darrell Gulin/Getty Images, pp. 24–25; Justin Lewis/Getty Images, p. 26; Michael Nolan/Getty Images, p. 27; Jeff Foott/Getty Images, p. 28. Design elements: Cassel/Shutterstock; iunewind/Shutterstock; Milano M/Shutterstock; Print Net/Shutterstock; Textures and backgrounds/Shutterstock; Ukrainian studio/Shutterstock.

Cover: Gabrielle Therin-Weise/Getty Images; Paul Souders/Getty Images.